SCOTLAND SINCE 1900

RICHARD DARGIE

Explore Scottish History is packed with historical evidence to help you discover how Scotland's people lived in the past. It also includes links to the Heinemann Explore website and CD-ROM ⊙.

Heinemann
LIBRARY

H www.heinemann.co.uk/library
Visit our website to find out more information about Heinemann Library books.

To order:
☎ Phone 44 (0) 1865 888066
📄 Send a fax to 44 (0) 1865 314091
💻 Visit the Heinemann Library Bookshop at www.heinemann.co.uk/library to browse our catalogue and order online.

First published in Great Britain by Heinemann Library, Halley Court, Jordan Hill, Oxford OX2 8EJ, a division of Reed Educational and Professional Publishing Ltd. Heinemann is a registered trademark of Reed Educational & Professional Publishing Ltd.

OXFORD MELBOURNE AUCKLAND JOHANNESBURG BLANTYRE
GABORONE IBADAN PORTSMOUTH (NH) USA CHICAGO

Designed by Celia Floyd
Originated by Dot Gradations
Printed by Wing King Tong in Hong Kong

06 05 04 03 02
10 9 8 7 6 5 4 3 2 1

ISBN 0 431 14530 X (hardback)

06 05 04 03 02
10 9 8 7 6 5 4 3 2 1

ISBN 0 431 14531 8 (paperback)

British Library Cataloguing in Publication Data

Dargie, Richard
   Scotland since 1900. – (Explore Scottish history)
   1. Scotland – History – 20th century – Juvenile literature
   I. Title
   941.1'082

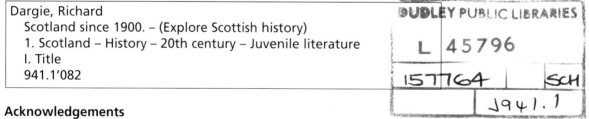

Acknowledgements

The Publishers would like to thank the following for permission to reproduce photographs:

AKG photos p11, Corbis pp23, 25, Hulton Getty pp5, 6, 9, 12, 13, 14, 15, 16, 18, 20, 21, 22, 24, 26, 28, Scotland in Focus pp8, 19, 27, 29, SCRAN p10 (The Scotsman Publications).

Cover photograph reproduced with permission of SMN Archive (Glasgow Herald).

Our thanks to Ian Hall of the University of St Andrews for his comments during the writing of this book.

Every effort has been made to contact copyright holders of any material reproduced in this book. Any omissions will be rectified in subsequent printings if notice is given to the Publisher.

Any words appearing in the text in bold, **like this**, are explained in the glossary.

Contents

Scotland in 1900

In 1900 Scotland was one of the richest countries in the world. Scotland's factories produced thousands of goods that were sent all over the world. Many Scottish workers were highly skilled; they earned good wages and took great pride in their work. Scottish ships, railways, engines and other products were highly prized overseas.

Many Scots were also proud to be British. Britain controlled the biggest **Empire** the world had ever seen. The Union flag flew over a hundred British territories scattered across every continent. Scots had played a big part in winning the Empire in the nineteenth century, and many of them now helped to run it.

Not all Scots shared in the country's wealth and prestige. In 1900 there was a huge difference between the lives of the rich and the poor. Life was very comfortable for the upper and middle classes. However, many unskilled working-class Scots had hard jobs, low wages and poor housing. Although the worst of the slums had been cleared, and town councils had worked hard to provide fresh running water and sewage pipes to most homes, life was still tough for most Scottish mine and mill workers.

In the years after 1900 life in Scotland began to change very quickly. The rich had telephones and electricity in their homes for the first time, and aeroplanes flew across Scotland. Women also wanted a bigger say in how the country was run, and workers were demanding better wages and conditions. Scotland was entering a new age.

The motor car was the symbol of the new, modern Scotland. In 1898 there were only about a hundred cars in Scotland, all owned by a few rich men. By 1914 however there were ten thousand cars in the country, and ordinary people like doctors and lawyers drove cars to work. A large car factory, the Argyll Motor Works, had been built at Alexandria, north of Glasgow.

In 1901 Queen Victoria died and her son became King Edward VII. He only reigned for nine years but they were years of prosperity and jollity for many Scots. Britain and Scotland had never seemed so strong and powerful. Yet Britain's wealth and confidence made its rivals, such as Germany, very jealous. In 1914 Britain and Germany began a bitter war that lasted for more than four years.

From a speech by a Scottish politician in 1901

"Britain enters the new century more confident than ever before in its long history. The Empire is prosperous and at peace. The rest of the world looks to us for leadership. This new age will be a glorious one for Britain and for Scotland."

Exploring further

The Heinemann Explore CD-ROM will give you extra information about Scotland, Britain and the wider world during the twentieth century. From the Contents screen click on the blue words to find out more.

Votes for Scottish women!

Women in Scotland had few rights in 1900. Working-class women often had to work very long hours but earned less than men. Educated middle-class women found it difficult to get jobs as doctors and lawyers. Although some could vote in local elections, women could not vote in elections for Members of Parliament.

Most men expected women to stay at home as wives and mothers. However, new technology such as typewriters and the telephone created new kinds of jobs in offices. After 1872, all Scottish girls got a good education up to the age of thirteen and were well suited for these new jobs. Women were earning better wages but they also wanted equal voting rights or **suffrage**.

Scottish women played a big part in the campaign for the right to vote. The Women's Social and Political Union (WSPU), which campaigned for female suffrage, held impressive demonstrations in Edinburgh in 1907 and 1909. The main organizer of the WSPU in London was Flora Drummond from Arran. She was nicknamed, 'The General', and even rode on horseback at the head of several 'suffragette' demonstrations.

Flora Drummond was arrested at a WSPU rally in London in 1914

After 1910 some Scottish suffragette campaigners turned to violence, trying to force the all-male government in London to give them the vote. Ethel Moorhead from Dundee set fire to pillar boxes and smashed shop windows. The suffragettes were also blamed for serious fires at Kelso and Ayr racecourses.

Even powerful men were not safe from the suffragettes. The Prime Minister was attacked while he was on a golfing holiday in Lossiemouth, and four suffragettes with whips and red pepper also attacked him as he drove through Bannockburn. Scottish suffragettes slashed a portrait of the King in the main art gallery in Edinburgh. Others crept on to his private golf course at Balmoral Castle and replaced the marker flags with pennants in the green and purple colours of the WSPU. Suffragettes threw eggs at Winston Churchill, then Home Secretary, when he visited Dundee.

Many leading suffragettes were arrested for these violent protests. When they went on **hunger strike** in prison, the government ordered force-feeding. Ethel Moorhead was the first Scottish woman to suffer this painful and dangerous process at the Calton Jail in Edinburgh. In February 1914 tubes were forced down her throat and food was pumped into her stomach. Despite their campaigns and sacrifices however, Scottish women were no nearer getting the vote when war broke out later that year.

"I helped blow up the pillar box at the top of Market Street. We stuffed in a rag soaked in paraffin and then threw in a match. We wanted to burn the mail belonging to the banks and companies that used the Royal Mail, so they would tell the government to give us the vote."

From the memories of an Aberdeen suffragette

Exploring further – The Changing Role of Women

It was not only Scottish women who battled to be able to vote. This issue was a major concern in England and across the world. Follow this path on the CD-ROM to discover more:
Digging Deeper > Modern Britain > Votes for Women.

Scots at war

In the summer of 1914, Britain went to war against Germany and her allies. Scots played an important part in the war. Like people throughout Europe, they thought the war was a great adventure and would only last a few months. Instead the Great War dragged on for over four years and cost millions of lives thanks to new deadly weapons such as machine guns, high explosive shells and barbed wire.

Many Scots joined the army in the first months of the war, often **enlisting** with their friends. Over a thousand men who worked together on Glasgow's trams joined in one 'pals battalion'. There were so many Scottish recruits that the army ran out of uniforms, boots and rifles for them. Throughout the winter of 1914 and the first months of 1915, Scotland was covered in regimental camps where the new troops learned how to become soldiers.

The front line

Many Scottish troops were sent to the **Western Front** in Flanders and France. Here they faced all the dangers of the front line trenches such as constant shelling and poison gas. They were also badly tormented by lice, which liked to lay their eggs in the folds of the heavy kilts worn by most Scottish soldiers. However, the Germans feared 'the soldiers in skirts' and trembled when they heard the unearthly sound of approaching bagpipes.

Field Marshal Sir Douglas Haig

For much of the war, Britain's top commander was the Scot, Field Marshal Sir Douglas Haig. He believed he could win the war by breaking through the well-defended German trenches. Haig planned a huge attack on the Germans along the river Somme in July 1916. He put many Scottish units in the front line of the attack because he thought they were the best troops in his army. Unfortunately this meant that Scotland suffered very heavy losses when the Battle of the Somme ended in defeat.

Scottish regiments also suffered badly at the Battle of Passchendaele in 1917, where many soldiers drowned in a sea of mud. Many others were killed in the disastrous campaign at Gallipoli in Turkey. Almost every family in Scotland was touched by the war, losing a father, brother or son. After the war every village and town in Scotland recorded the names of the dead on their own war memorial. Many people were angry that the government in London had thrown away the lives of so many Scots.

These Scottish recruits were typical of the thousands who 'joined up' in 1915.

From the memoirs of a Gordon Highlander

"I was in the first wave that crossed into no-mans-land at 7.30 am precisely on July 1st, 1916. I was stretchered out at exactly 7.53 with most of my left knee-cap and shin blown away by German machine-gun fire. But I wasn't too unhappy. Losing half a leg wasn't much of a price to pay to get home and out of the war."

Exploring further – First World War

The war had a huge effect on the people of Scotland. Follow this path to find out how many Scots were killed in the war:
Written Sources > The number of people who died in World War One
Many more people were maimed for life.

Scotswomen at war

The lives of ordinary women in Scotland were greatly affected by the Great War of 1914–1918. As so many men were away fighting in the war, women had to take on new kinds of jobs to keep the country going. Women were soon working on the trams and buses of Scotland's cities as drivers and conductors. Others acquired new skills learning to build much needed ships in the Clydeside shipyards, or making weapons at the huge **ammunition** and explosives factory at Gretna in southern Scotland.

As soon as war broke, most of the suffragettes stopped campaigning for the vote, and took up war work instead. Many active suffragettes knew that poorer families were suffering badly with their wage-earning menfolk away at war. They set up Scottish Women's War Relief Committees in every part of the country, helping families to find enough food, coal and clothing. Other suffragettes became nurses to help with the huge numbers of war wounded.

Dr Elsie Inglis

Dr Elsie Inglis was a doctor in Edinburgh who planned to set up teams of well-trained women who could act as doctors, nurses and ambulance drivers in France. However the government in London thought she was interfering and had no time for her ideas. So Elsie came back to Scotland, raised the money and trained the women herself. In 1915 she sent her first teams to Serbia and France. They worked until the end of the war, saving thousands of lives. Elsie herself died before the war ended, worn out by working so hard to save others.

New freedoms

Women like Elsie Inglis proved that they were the equal of any man, and could play a full part in running the country. In 1918 the government gave the vote to women over the age of 30. Ten years later, all adult women over twenty-one had this important right.

The war changed women in other ways. Many worked away from home and had a taste of freedom from their families for the first time. Others enjoyed the high wages they earned which they could often spend on themselves. After the Great War, women went out more on their own or with friends, and did daring things like smoking in public.

A Dundee woman remembers the wages she earned in 1918

"When there were long shifts, you got time and a half and could up your wages. Twice I earned over a fiver for a week's work. That was big wages then. I'd been in service in a doctor's house as a maid before the war and thought I was well enough paid at around a pound a week."

With the men away at war, it was up to the women to work in ammunitions factories, like this one, making weapons.

Exploring further – Amy Johnson

The First World War made a huge difference to women's lives across Britain. Read about one pioneering woman on the CD-ROM. Follow this path:

Biographies > Amy Johnson.

The Great Slump

During the Great War, Scotland's factories were busy producing weapons, uniforms, ships and other war supplies. There was plenty of work for all and wages were high. These boom years carried on after peace came in 1918 as countries around the world replaced the things destroyed by years of war.

However, after 1921 many Scottish companies began to run out of orders and had to lay off their workers. Scottish factories were still making old-fashioned things such as steam **locomotives**. They didn't make the modern products such as radios and motor cars which people wanted after the war. Many of Scotland's customers abroad had also found other, cheaper suppliers during the war years.

Many Scots went on 'Hunger Marches' during the years of Depression to protest at the lack of jobs in Scotland.

The 1920s and early 1930s were tough years for the Scottish economy. Thousands of workers were unemployed and even for those in a job, wages were low. Times were especially hard for the many wounded men who came back from the Great War and found it difficult to get work. Things became even worse after the American Wall Street Crash in 1929 that set off a **Depression** in world trade. There was even less demand for Scottish products, and in parts of the **Central Belt** the unemployment rate was over 30 per cent by 1934. Many working class Scottish families endured years of desperate poverty.

Some of the unemployed did get help from the government. There were schemes of National Assistance that paid a weekly benefit. However, the sums were small and were reduced if a family had any income of its own. Even a child's earnings on a paper round were taken into account in these calculations.

Not everyone was prepared to stand in line waiting for a job. Almost four hundred thousand Scots **emigrated** to other countries hoping to find a job and a better life in Canada or Australia. Advertisements for shipping companies offered cheap passage to the **colonies** but didn't mention that things were tough there as well. Nevertheless, so many people left Scotland during the years of Slump and Depression that Scotland's population fell for the first time since 1750. Not surprisingly, many Scots felt that things in Scotland needed to be changed.

Scottish emigrants enjoy a Highland jig as they sail to Canada in 1926.

Unemployment rate in Scotland, 1918–1932	1918	2%	1929	12%
	1920	3%	1931	27%
	1925	8%	1932	28%

Exploring further – John Logie Baird

The 1930s were a tough time for many Scots, but Scottish inventors like John Logie Baird were still having a great influence around the world. Find out more about Baird on the CD-ROM:
Biographies > John Logie Baird.

Slump politics

At the start of the twentieth century, most Scottish voters supported the Liberal Party. There were important Liberal governments in the early years of the century. They introduced reforms such as the Old Age Pension, and led Britain to victory over Germany in the First World War or 'Great War'.

However many Scots wanted the government to do more for ordinary people. As members of **trade unions**, they helped to found the Labour Party in 1900. Its aim was to win more power for working-class people, and give a bigger share of the country's wealth to the poor.

From the beginning, Scots played a big part in the Labour movement. This was especially the case on Clydeside around Glasgow where workers had long felt they were poorly paid for their skills. There were even strikes in factories and shipyards there during the First World War. Two great Clydesiders in the early Labour movement, Willie Gallacher and Emmanuel Shinwell, were arrested in 1919 when the government feared that a **revolution** was breaking out in Glasgow.

Nevertheless, many Scots voted for the new Labour Party and helped it to win power in 1924 and 1929. By 1930 there were also many Labour town councils across Scotland that built new estates of council houses. These gave poor families the chance of a decent house at a reasonably cheap rent.

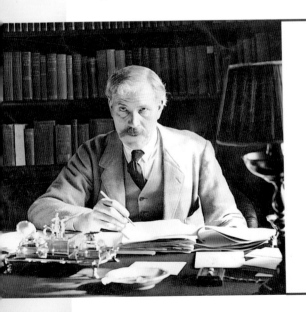

James Ramsay MacDonald

The 1929 Labour Government had many Scottish MPs and even a Scottish Prime Minister, James Ramsay MacDonald from Lossiemouth. Across Scotland, people hoped that this new government could solve the problems of the Slump. However in 1931, MacDonald split the Labour Party. At the height of the Depression crisis, he formed a government of national unity with the Conservatives. Many Scots at the time felt that MacDonald was a traitor to their cause.

The long years of Slump and **Depression** made many Scots think about how Scotland was governed. It seemed to them that Scotland was neglected by the government 400 miles away in England. They believed that Scotland needed **Home Rule** or independence, as a government in Edinburgh would take more interest in Scottish problems.

In 1934 the Scottish National Party or SNP was formed to campaign for Scottish independence. Many of the SNP's founders had been in the Labour movement such as the MP Robert Cunninghame Graham. The government wanted to show it was listening to the Scots, and two years later the Scottish Office was moved from London to Edinburgh.

 From an early SNP pamphlet written in 1936

"Around the globe people in countries large and small look to their governments for help to solve the problems of the Great Depression. Only the Scots must look to a government in another land and hope that it will not neglect them. The solution to Scottish problems must be Scottish Home Rule."

Exploring further – Adolf Hitler

The Great Depression affected politics in other countries as well.
Read about Hitler's rise to power in Germany on the CD-ROM:

Digging Deeper > Adolf Hitler.

At work and play

Throughout the early 1930s, the huge unfinished hull of an ocean liner towered above the river Clyde. This was Order 534, planned as one of the biggest ships ever built anywhere in the world. Its owner was the Cunard shipping company, which had run out of money in the **Depression** crisis in 1931. For four years the vast hull cast a shadow across Clydebank and was a daily reminder of Scotland's deep problems.

However David Kirkwood, the Labour MP for Clydebank, would not let the ship rust away. He persuaded the government to help Cunard with loans to finish the work. Thousands of men in the Glasgow area were soon employed on Order 534, which was launched as the *Queen Mary* in 1934.

The government also made central Scotland a 'Special Area'. New industrial estates were opened such as Hillington near Renfrew. It had modern factories that used electricity rather than the old steam power. After 1935, orders slowly began to come in for Scotland's factories and there were jobs and money to spare. The popular song of the day was called "*Happy days are here again*". However the reason for the jobs was not a happy one. Fear of Hitler's Germany meant that the government had started to stockpile weapons in case of a future war.

A Clydebank shipfitter

"I was on slow-time and the dole for almost three years until the *Queen Mary* got going again. Then there was a need for all kinds of skilled men that had just been cooling their heels. The whole town and all of Scotland got a lift from the *Queen Mary*. There was a bit of hope again."

Throughout the 1930s, people in Scotland found an escape from their worries by 'going to the pictures' or cinema. Every town had at least one Picture Palace that showed the latest movies from Hollywood, as well as British-made films. Aberdeen had almost 30 cinema houses while Glasgow had 50. Many people went to the pictures several times a week.

Cinema houses often had glamorous sounding names such as The Astoria or The Majestic, and were elaborate and glittering inside. The staff dressed up in smart uniforms to add to the feeling of a special occasion. The films themselves were often romantic and spectacular and took the audience far away from their own troubled lives.

Others took pleasure in football. This was the great age of Scottish 'fitba'. There were many strong teams in the Scottish First Division and Scottish players also starred in the top English sides. Attendances at football matches were huge in the 1930s. Almost one hundred and fifty thousand people crushed into Hampden in April 1937 to watch Scotland beat England 3:1. Only a few days later, another massive crowd of one hundred and forty-six thousand watched Aberdeen and Celtic in the Scottish Cup Final.

An Edinburgh woman remembers going to the cinema in the 1930s

"Going to the pictures was just magic. From the minute you went in, you were treated special by the cinema staff; they called you Madam and showed you to your seat. The whole place was plush with deep red carpets, velvet seats and chandeliers. These were things most people had never even seen before, let alone have in their homes."

Exploring further – Changes in work

Work in Britain has changed a lot since the Great Depression. Follow this path on the CD-ROM to find out more:

Exploring the Wider World > Focus On: Changes in Britain since 1930 > Work.

Scotland and the Second World War

In the late summer of 1939 war broke out again in Europe when Hitler's Germany invaded Poland. As Britain had promised to help the Poles, Britain declared war on Germany on 3rd September. For the second time in twenty years, Scots found themselves in uniform and taking part in the national war effort.

Scotland was vital to Britain's survival in the war against Germany. Hitler planned to starve Britain into surrendering using his submarines or **U-boats** to sink all ships carrying supplies to this island. The Clyde became an important waterway where convoys of ships gathered before setting out to get supplies from America. After 1941, convoys also used Loch Broom near Ullapool as a shelter before making the hazardous journey north to the Arctic ports of our Russian **Allies**.

For much of the war, the ports at Greenock, Dumbarton and Clydebank were important Allied harbours. Here Allied ships could unload troops and supplies reasonably safely, out of range of most, though not all, enemy bombers. The Royal Navy based its northern fleet at Scapa Flow in the Orkneys. Only a month into the war, the battleship *Royal Oak* was sunk here in a surprise U-boat attack with over eight hundred lives lost in minutes.

In 1940 the Germans occupied Norway and Denmark. This put Scotland in the front line as German planes could now reach much of Scotland from across the North Sea. The Royal Air Force and the Royal Navy built a string of air bases around Scotland's coast. The Germans photographed the Forth Rail Bridge and regularly bombed the shipyards in Aberdeen Harbour.

Even civilians suffered when the Germans bombed the Royal Navy in the Orkneys.

It had been obvious for some months that a war was likely, and many men volunteered to join the army even before war broke out. However, after September 1939 all men of military age were **conscripted** or called up to the Armed Forces. As in 1914, Scotland was covered with makeshift camps and barracks as thousands of soldiers were toughened up in Scotland's wild countryside.

Northern Scotland was an ideal place to train soldiers. The first **commandos** were trained at Ardnamurchan and at Spean Bridge in the Western Highlands. At Glen More near Aviemore, Norwegians who escaped to Scotland were taught how to use explosives. They then went back to their own country to fight the Germans as secret agents and **saboteurs**. The Norwegian flag still flies at Glen More in memory of these brave men and women.

This statue at Spean Bridge remembers the commandos who trained in the Highlands.

Exploring further – Key people

The Biographies section of the CD-ROM tells you about many of the important people of the Second World War, including Neville Chamberlain, Winston Churchill and Adolf Hitler.

Scots against Hitler

In May 1940, Hitler launched an all-out attack on France and conquered it in a few short weeks. The British army in France was quickly surrounded and had to retreat and try to escape back to England. Almost three hundred thousand British troops were soon trapped on the beaches near the port of Dunkirk. Thousands of weary, defeated men were safely carried back across the English Channel by hundreds of small ships and boats.

Troops waited patiently in line to be picked off the Dunkirk beaches.

The 51st Highland Division was the main Scottish part of this army. It was ordered to keep fighting back the Germans and to win time so that the rest of the army could escape. Armed with rifles, they were asked to take on Hitler's **panzers** and Stuka dive-bombers. Outnumbered and outgunned, the 51st Division fought for days until the last of the beaches was cleared.

They suffered very heavy losses but their brave sacrifice made the miracle of Dunkirk possible. The survivors had to spend five years in German prisoner-of-war camps. There they kept up their spirits by inventing new Highland dances and trying to escape. A Gaelic memorial at St Valery on the French coast commemorates their exceptional bravery.

Scots served in all the theatres of war after 1940. Some were stationed in India and fought the Japanese in the steaming jungles of Burma. Many Gordon Highlanders were captured in the Fall of Singapore in 1942. However the pipes led Scottish regiments to victory in North Africa in the same year and in Italy in 1943. Fittingly, it was a new 51st Highland Division made up of fresh recruits that played a big part in these successes.

Sir Fitzroy Maclean

Sir Fitzroy Maclean was one of the most famous Scottish soldiers of the war. He was trained as a **commando** secret agent and parachuted behind enemy lines into German occupied Yugoslavia. There he helped organize local resistance to the German army. He was later said to be the model for the spy James Bond in the novels written by Ian Fleming.

Not all Scots served in their traditional local regiments. Many joined the Royal Navy and the Royal Air Force, and fought alongside men from all over Britain and the British **Empire**. Others served in the Merchant Navy facing danger in the war against the German submarine fleet. Many of these men suffered terrible deaths when their ships were sunk in the icy waters of the North Atlantic Ocean.

Exploring further – The Blitz

Discover more about how the Blitz affected the people of Scotland and Britain.
Follow this path: Digging Deeper > The Blitz 1939 to 1945
Click on the topic headings to read about them.

The Home Front

The Second World War was a 'total war'. This means that every man, woman and child in the country was affected, not just the soldiers in battle. The people of Scotland discovered this in March 1941, when German bombers attacked the town of Clydebank in the worst **'blitz'** in Scotland.

The German bombers hoped to destroy the shipyards and weapons factories there but many of their bombs, dropped from over eight thousand feet, landed in the closely packed **tenements**. Over one thousand people were killed, and another two thousand were seriously injured.

Almost thirty-five thousand people were made homeless by the blitz and the fires that raged above Clydebank could be seen sixty miles away.

As soon as war began, **air raid shelters** were built across Scotland. Some of these were deep like the ones dug along Princes Street in Edinburgh. Some families just used Anderson shelter kits that cost seven pounds. They protected people from flying glass and **shrapnel** but were no use if you suffered a direct hit. In Glasgow, the closes between the tenements were turned into safe places by thick sandbags.

Before 1939 the government had already made plans to **evacuate** children from the cities to safer places in the countryside. Once the war began, thousands of children were moved from their homes. However, by late 1940 people realized that the blitz in Scotland was not as bad as they had feared. There were plenty of shelters and the strict **blackout** laws made it difficult for German bombers to find their targets. By 1941 most of Scotland's evacuees were back home again.

Food was a big problem for Scots on the Home Front. Everything was **rationed** and luxury foods from abroad such as sugar and chocolate were impossible to get. People had to grow as much of their own food as they could. Parks and gardens across Scotland were ploughed over and planted with potatoes, turnips and barley. People made old Scottish dishes such as haggis and **potted heid** to make the most of scraps of meat.

Scottish children also played their part in the war. The Boys Brigade and Girl Guides helped the wounded after air raids, or worked in hospitals as cleaners and cooks. Others collected valuable waste such as old tins and silver paper that could be used in the war effort. Many were awarded with the War Service Badge for their work.

From a Glasgow City Council evacuation letter to parents in March 1939

"The government are making plans to enable parents who live in the crowded areas of large cities to have their children transferred to safer places if war should ever break out. Older and younger members of each family will, as far as possible, be evacuated together. They will live in country houses where they will be welcome. They will go in the care of teachers who will remain with them."

Exploring further – Memories of war

We can learn a lot about the Second World War from the memories of the people who lived through it. You will find some of these memories in the Written sources section of the CD-ROM, along with other memories of the twentieth century.

The post-war boom

In 1945 Labour won a landslide victory in the General Election. Most Scots hoped that the new Labour government would solve Scotland's many problems such as poor housing. Some felt that the government in London was too distant from Scotland.

In the years between 1945 and 1965, both Labour and Conservative governments built record numbers of houses. Many Scottish families moved from city slums to new houses in the **suburbs** with front and back gardens. This was just one sign of Scotland's growing prosperity in the post-war boom. In 1945 only wealthy people owned a car, but by the late 1960s most Scottish families had one parked on the street in front of their house. Motor cars gave Scottish people a personal freedom in their lives that they had never had before.

New towns such as Glenrothes in Fife were a sign of the hopes for the future which people had at this time. Many of the people who moved to Glenrothes were coalworkers who had long suffered terrible working and living conditions. Glenrothes was a model town with modern shops, wide attractive streets, green open spaces and gardens, and neat rows of well-built houses. Other successful new towns followed at Cumbernauld, Irvine and Livingston.

There were also new kinds of jobs in Scotland as the government tried to encourage new industries. A huge car plant was opened in 1963 at Linwood near Paisley, employing thousands of workers. An **aluminium smelter** was opened at Invergordon in the Highlands in 1968 to encourage people to stay in the north. The symbol of this new Scotland was the **nuclear reactor** at Dounreay in Caithness. Scotland's old industries of iron and coal were fading, but it seemed they would easily be replaced by new ways of making wealth.

After 1955 people found they had more money to spend on themselves and their homes. They were able to buy modern furniture and new gadgets such as televisions and washing machines. Travelling abroad to warm countries such as Spain and Italy became more common after 1960 thanks to companies that offered package holiday deals. The Scots were becoming part of the 'consumer society'.

However the Scots were now also part of a new global society. Young Scots, like young people everywhere, became interested in fashion and music from around the world and especially America. Older Scottish traditions were in danger of being neglected.

The fashion and music of 'rock and roll' stars like Elvis Presley caught the imagination of young people all around the world.

Exploring further – Teenagers

Teenage culture grew in the 1950s, as part of the post-war boom.
Read more about this new social group on the CD-ROM:
Exploring Scotland > Discoveries, Inventions and Ideas > Teenagers
You can also see pictures of teenagers from the time.

Years of change, 1975–2000

Scotland saw many changes in the last years of the twentieth century. The great shipyards on the Clyde either closed or merged during the 1970s, and most of Scotland's coal mines closed down after the Miners' Strike in 1984. The giant Ravenscraig Steel Works near Motherwell also closed after much public protest.

The plans to close Ravenscraig sparked off many bitter protests in Scotland.

Scotland's traditional industries had struggled for many years. Other countries such as Japan could make cheaper products than Scotland. However many Scots felt that the government in London did little to help them. From 1979 to 1997 the Conservatives were in government. They did not think it was worth protecting Scotland's old industries, and this angered many Scots. Scotland wasn't getting the kind of government that it voted for, and this made many Scots argue for a greater measure of **Home Rule**.

Oil

Not all of Scotland's industries were old or dying. In 1969, vast reserves of oil were discovered off Scotland's coast. The oil itself was worth billions of pounds but it also created a tremendous boom in jobs. Vast drilling platforms were built at Ardersier near Inverness, and at Applecross in Wester Ross. These were towed to the North Sea oil fields and became the temporary home of 'riggers and roughnecks'.

Aberdeen became the oil capital of Europe as workers flooded into the area. Dyce Airport near the city became the busiest in the world as hundreds of helicopters daily carried men and supplies to the North Sea rigs. However, finding oil in the deep North Sea was a dangerous business and there were many accidents on the rigs. The worst came when the Piper Alpha rig exploded on July 6 1988, killing 167 men.

New industry

There were also new industries in Central Scotland. Many high-tech electronic companies built modern factories along the M8 corridor between Glasgow and Edinburgh. They made valuable new products such as computers and mobile phones.

After 1973 Scotland was part of the **Common Market** and then the **European Union**. More of Scotland's trade was with Europe rather than North America. Fewer people now lived in Glasgow, while the towns and cities on the East Coast nearest to Europe grew in size. By 2015, the population of Edinburgh was expected to overtake Glasgow again for the first time since the 1750s.

From the *Glasgow Herald* in 1992

"Today's announcement that another major electronics firm is moving into Silicon Glen is very welcome news for Scotland. The initial 400 jobs are in assembling products, and in distribution but the company has given a commitment to using Scotland as a base for the more important phases of research and development."

Exploring further – Technology

One of the main reasons for change in Scotland and around the world has been the growth of new technology. Follow this path on the CD-ROM to read more: Exploring the Wider World > Focus On: Changes in Britain since 1930 > Technology.

A new Scottish Parliament

Although it was founded in 1934, the SNP had little success in its first 30 years. During the Second World War and afterwards, most Scots were still happy to think of themselves as British. They felt that the governments in London were doing a good enough job for Scotland. Then in 1967, a young lawyer called Winnie Ewing won a stunning victory for the SNP in the Hamilton by-election. Scotland would never be the same again.

SNP supporters accompanied Winnie Ewing to London when she entered the House of Commons.

Like many Scots in the late 1960s, the Hamilton voters felt that they had been neglected and taken for granted by the Labour government in London. They cast a protest vote for the SNP. The discovery of vast oil riches in the North Sea added to the success of the SNP, because many Scots feared that the government in London would not use this great wealth wisely.

Soon the SNP slogan, 'It's Scotland's Oil', was on every hoarding. In the election of 1974 the SNP won eleven seats in the Westminster Parliament and over 30 per cent of the votes cast. Although the SNP vote slipped back in later elections, they became Scotland's second political party after Labour, and a great debate broke out about how Scotland could best be governed.

At the same time many Scots found a new sense of national identity. There was much more interest in Scottish traditions in music, language and the arts. New technology meant that many more books and films were made in, and about Scotland. Scots seemed to have found a new confidence in themselves.

The Labour Party won the 1997 UK General Election in a landslide. They had promised to set up a strong Scottish Parliament in Edinburgh. The Conservatives, who were strongly against this idea, lost all their MPs in Scotland. In a **referendum**, the Scots voted overwhelmingly for their new Parliament, and the way was open for a historic change.

The first Scottish Parliament since 1707 met in Edinburgh in 1999. Labour had won the Scottish Elections, and it formed the first Scottish Executive or government under the Scottish First Minister Donald Dewar. Fittingly, the new Parliament was opened by Winnie Ewing, the SNP victor in 1967. Many Scots felt that a new age was beginning for their country.

 Sadly Donald Dewar died suddenly in 2000. However in his few short months as Scotland's First Minister, he set in motion the construction of a new building for Scotland's lawmakers. The new Scottish Parliament set in the heart of Edinburgh's Old Town at Holyrood, is planned to open in 2003.

Exploring further – Searching the twentieth century

To find more information about the twentieth century click on Search on the top panel of the Contents page. Pick a word from the keywords on the next page and click on Enter. The screen will now show a list of pages on the CD-ROM that mention this word. Click on the names of the pages to find out what they show.

Timeline

1901	Death of Queen Victoria
1907	Suffragette demonstrations start in Edinburgh
1914	The Great War – Britain goes to war against Germany in the First World War
1916	Battle of the Somme – Scots regiments suffer appalling losses
1917	Battle of Passchendaele – more Scots regiments' casualties
1918	Government gives women over the age of 30 the right to vote
1920s	The Great Slump – economic **Depression** hits Scotland
1928	Women over the age of 21 are given the right to vote
1929	American Wall Street Crash – the stock market in America collapses adding to worldwide economic Depression
1930s	Scots **emigrate** in vast numbers, and Scotland's population falls for the first time since 1750
1931	Scottish Labour Prime Minister James Ramsay MacDonald forms a government of national unity with the Conservatives
1934	SNP formed
1934	*Queen Mary* (Order 534) finally launched
1939	Hitler invades Poland – 3 September Britain declares war against Germany
1940	Battle of Dunkirk
1941	German Luftwaffe **blitz** Clydebank
1945	Labour win a landslide victory in General Election
1963	Car plant opens at Linwood near Paisley providing much needed jobs
1967	SNP win first parliamentary seat in Hamilton by-election
1968	**Aluminium smelter** at Invergordon opens providing jobs for the Highlands
1969	Oil reserves discovered off Scotland's coast
1973	Scotland becomes part of the **Common Market** (later the **European Union**)
1984	Miner's Strike. Ravenscraig Steel Works later closed with the loss of thousands of jobs.
1988	Piper Alpha oil rig explodes causing deaths of 167 men
1999	First Scottish Parliament since 1707 meets in Edinburgh

Glossary

air raid shelters   where people took shelter during the bombing raids of the Second World War

Allies   countries supporting Britain in the Second World War

aluminium smelter   industrial furnace where aluminium is made

ammunition   bullets and shells used by modern weapons

blackout   keeping all lights hidden at night so that enemy pilots couldn't see their targets

blitz   heavy bombing of cities in the Second World War, named after the German word for lightning

Central Belt   part of Scotland between Glasgow and Edinburgh

colonies   countries that are part of an empire

commando   special soldier trained to fight behind enemy lines

Common Market   name given to the European Union in the 1960s and 70s

conscripted   ordered to join the army by the government

consumer society   when everyone wants to buy many products

Depression   years of poverty and unemployment between 1929 and 1935

emigrate   leave your own country to live in another

Empire   group of states ruled by a single government

enlisting   volunteering to join the army

European Union   union of fifteen countries in Western Europe

evacuate   to send someone away from a place of danger

Home Rule   the wish of people in Scotland, Ireland and Wales to run their own countries

hunger strike   when prisoners refuse to eat or drink

locomotives   steam engines that power railways

nuclear reactor   power plant or factory which makes electricity from atomic fuel

panzers   heavy German tanks used in the Second World War

potted heid   dish eaten in Scotland made from meat scraps in jelly

rationed   when food and other supplies are shared out equally to everybody during wartime

referendum   national vote on an important issue

revolution   sudden change which affects peoples lives dramatically

saboteur   secret agent who blows up railway lines, bridges and factories in wartime

shrapnel   bits of metal that fly off when a bomb explodes

suburbs   housing areas on the edge of a town or city

suffrage   the right to vote

tenements   high buildings divided up into flats

trade union   workers who join together to fight for higher wages and better working conditions

U-boats   German submarines in both World Wars

Western Front   line of trenches in France and Belgium, the site of many battles of the First World War

Index

Titles in the *Explore Scottish History* series include:

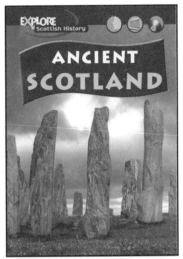

Hardback   0 431 14520 2

Hardback   0 431 14522 9

Hardback   0 431 14524 5

Hardback   0 431 14526 1

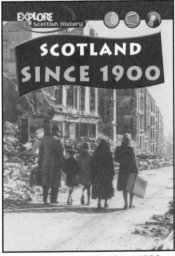

Hardback   0 431 14530 x

Find out about the other titles in this series on our website www.heinemann.co.uk/library

Alien Neighbours?

Angela Royston

www.raintreepublishers.co.uk

Visit our website to find out more information about **Raintree** books.

To order:
☎ Phone 44 (0) 1865 888112
▤ Send a fax to 44 (0) 1865 314091
▯ Visit the Raintree bookshop at **www.raintreepublishers.co.uk** to browse our catalogue and order online.

First published in Great Britain by Raintree,
Halley Court, Jordan Hill, Oxford OX2 8EJ,
part of Harcourt Education.
Raintree is a registered trademark of Harcourt
Education Ltd.

Editorial: Lucy Thunder, Charlotte Guillain,
and Harriet Milles
Design: Victoria Bevan and Bigtop
Illustrations: Darren Lingard and John Haslam
Picture Research: Melissa Allison and Fiona Orbell
Production: Camilla Crask

Originated by Dot Gradations Ltd
Printed and bound in Italy by Printer Trento srl

The paper used to print this book comes from
sustainable resources.

ISBN 1 844 43854 6
10 09 08 07 06
10 9 8 7 6 5 4 3 2 1

British Library Cataloguing in Publication Data
Royston, Angela
Alien Neighbours?: The Solar System
523.2
A full catalogue record for this book is available from
the British Library.

Acknowledgements
The publishers would like to thank the following
for permission to reproduce photographs:
Corbis/NASA/Roger Ressmeyer pp. **10–11**, **17**, **25**
(lower); Corbis/ZUMA/Cornell/JPL/NASA pp. **12–13**;
NASA Kennedy Space Center (NASA-KSC) p. **7**;
Science Photo Library/David A. Hardy, Futures:
50 Years in Space pp. **18–19**; Science Photo
Library/Detlev Van Ravenswaay pp. **22–23**, **25** (top),
26–27; Science Photo Library/Joe Tucciarone
pp. **14–15**; Science Photo Library/NASA pp. **4**, **8–9**;
Science Photo Library/NASA/Space Telescope
Science Centre pp. **20–21**.

Cover photograph of water on Mars, reproduced
with permission of Science Photo Library/Detlev
Van Ravenswaay.

Every effort has been made to contact copyright
holders of any material reproduced in this book.
Any omissions will be rectified in subsequent
printings if notice is given to the publishers.

The publishers would like to thank Nancy Harris
and Harold Pratt for their assistance in the
preparation of this book.

Contents

Some words are printed in bold, **like this**. You can find out what they mean on page 30. You can also look in the box at the bottom of the page where they first appear.

Looking for alien neighbours

Do we have alien neighbours in our **Solar System**? Is there life on the other **planets**? Are there **moons** that **orbit**, or circle, our Sun? Many scientists want to find out.

Spacecraft have already landed on some planets and moons. Spacecraft have flown past all the other planets, except Pluto. They have not found life – yet. But they have found water. They have also found a gas called **oxygen**. These are two things that living things need to survive.

What lies ▶ beyond Earth?

moon	object that orbits a planet
orbit	to circle around an object
oxygen	gas that living things need to survive
planet	object that orbits the Sun
Solar System	the Sun and everything that orbits it

No humans have travelled beyond the Earth's Moon. Would you like to be the first astronaut to explore the Solar System? You will visit many strange worlds. But do not expect to find creatures that can think and speak. What you are looking for are the smallest forms of life.

THE SOLAR SYSTEM

The Solar System includes the Sun and everything that circles around it. There are nine planets that orbit the Sun. Some have moons that circle around them.

The Solar System

Jupiter

Pluto

Sun

Mars

Earth

Asteroid Belt

Mercury

Uranus

Saturn

Venus

Neptune

The Moon

Your first stop is Earth's nearest neighbour – the **Moon**. The ground on Earth's Moon is bare rock. There are no plants or water. It is covered in craters. Craters are holes made by **meteorites**. Meteorites are lumps of rock. The meteorites crashed on to the Moon's surface and made craters.

There is no air on the Moon. This means there is no wind, or rain, or sound. Can you find any ice? Scientists think that ice could have come from a **comet**. A comet is a huge ball of ice. Comets **orbit** the Sun. An icy comet might have crashed into the Moon billions of years ago.

Ice is a form of water. It could contain tiny, simple forms of life called **microbes**. Take a sample of ice. Scientists will study the sample when you return to Earth.

HIGH JUMP

*You can jump six times higher on the Moon than you can on Earth! This is because **gravity** – the force that pulls you down to the ground – is less strong on the Moon than on Earth.*

comet	huge icy ball that orbits the Sun
gravity	force that pulls you down to the ground
meteorite	lump of rock that drifts through space
microbe	tiny, simple form of life that is too small to see without a microscope

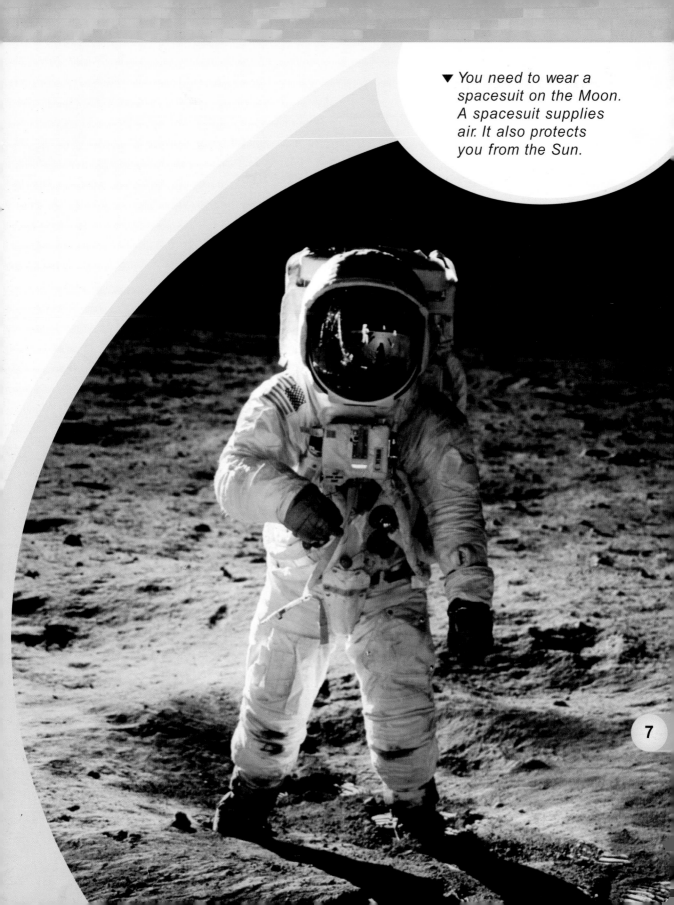

▼ *You need to wear a spacesuit on the Moon. A spacesuit supplies air. It also protects you from the Sun.*

Rocky planets

Mercury

The **planets** closest to the Sun are called the **inner planets**. They are made mostly of rock. Mercury is the nearest planet to the Sun. The Sun's rays are so strong here that they are deadly. Do not stay here long!

The strong sunshine heats up the ground. The temperature rises to 400 °C (752 °F). This is hot enough to melt heavy metal! But Mercury has almost no air around it to trap the heat. So night time on Mercury is freezing cold! The ground quickly cools to -200 °C (-328 °F).

The ground on Mercury has some deep cracks. These cracks are too deep to be warmed by the Sun. Scientists wonder if they are filled with ice. There could be tiny forms of life called **microbes** in the ice. Take a sample – but be quick!

SHORT YEARS

*Mercury has the shortest **year** of all the planets. Its year lasts only 88 Earth-days.*

inner planets   the four planets that are nearest to the Sun
year   length of time it takes a planet to orbit the Sun

Venus

Now you approach Venus. All you can see are thick clouds. Venus is about the same size as Earth. But Venus is very different from Earth. The **atmosphere** (gas) that surrounds Venus is poisonous. The gas is called carbon dioxide. The clouds are made of a poisonous liquid. This liquid is called sulphuric acid.

The clouds around Venus trap the Sun's heat. This makes Venus even hotter than Mercury! Be careful if you step outside. The atmosphere is so heavy it could crush your lungs! You will need armour under your spacesuit to protect you!

Venus

atmosphere	gases that surround a planet or moon
day	length of time it takes for a planet to spin around once

▼ The thick clouds around Venus block out the Sun's light. It would be hard to see much in the dim light.

11

LONGEST DAY

The planets all travel around the Sun. They also spin around like a spinning top. The time it takes for a **planet** to spin around once is called a **day**. A day on Venus lasts 243 Earth-days! This is longer than on any other planet.

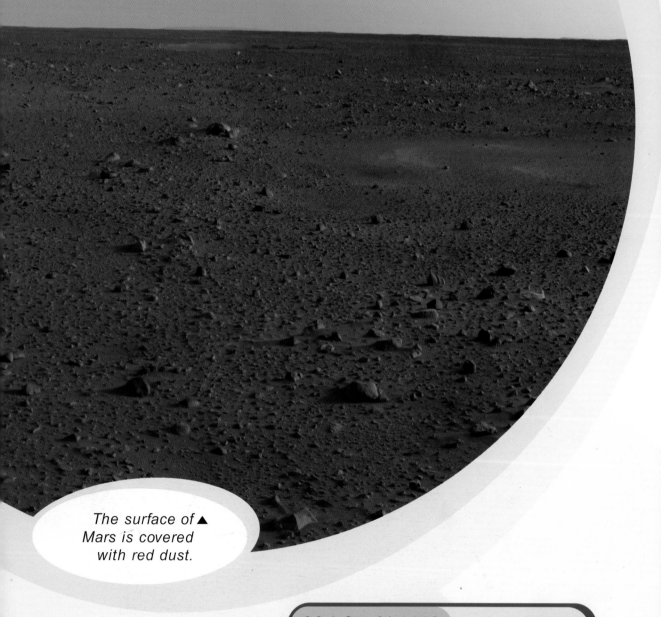

The surface of ▲
Mars is covered
with red dust.

SPACE PLANS

The US space agency is called NASA. It
wants to build a space station on Mars.
Space scientists hope to find water.
They also hope to find **microbes**.

extinct no longer active

Mars

Next stop – Mars. This is a rocky **planet**. Mars is about half the size of Earth. It has a warm summer (22 °C; 71 °F). But it is freezing cold in winter (-135 °C; -211 °F). The gases that surround Mars are poisonous too.

Mars has many huge, **extinct** volcanoes. This means that they no longer erupt. The highest is Olympus. It is the highest known mountain in the Universe!

The ground on Mars is covered with stones and red dust. Watch out when the wind begins to blow. The dust swirls around. It flies through the air. You are in the middle of a dust storm! You rush back to your spacecraft!

Mars

Dodging asteroids

Now it is time to leave the rocky **inner planets** behind. You head towards the **outer planets**. These planets are farther away from the Sun. You have to travel through thousands of **asteroids**.

Asteroids are chunks of rock. They form a broad area called the Asteroid Belt. Most asteroids are no bigger than boulders.

Steering the spacecraft through the Asteroid Belt is dangerous. Asteroids whizz past the spacecraft window. One nearly hits you!

MASSIVE CRASH

Asteroids sometimes break away from the Asteroid Belt. They crash into the **planets**. Scientists think that a large asteroid crashed into the Earth billions of years ago. Bits of Earth were blasted into space. These bits came together to form the **Moon**.

asteroid   large chunk of rock, or rock and metal, that orbits the Sun
outer planets   the five planets that are farthest from the Sun

▼ *Eros is one of the largest asteroids.*

Jupiter — the largest planet

Jupiter is huge. It is a thousand times bigger than Earth. It is the largest **planet** in the **Solar System**. You cannot land on Jupiter. It has no firm ground. Most of the planet is made of a light gas. This gas is called **hydrogen**. Beneath the thick hydrogen **atmosphere**, there is a deep ocean. What is the ocean made of? Liquid hydrogen!

Jupiter spins very fast as it travels round the Sun. It spins so fast that a **day** lasts less than ten hours. This fast·spin whips up strong winds.

Jupiter

hydrogen   gas that is much lighter than air

Do not fly too close to Jupiter. If you do, you will get sucked in. You will be smashed to bits by the high winds. Instead, you can explore Europa. Europa is one of Jupiter's **moons**.

Great Red Spot

MOONS

Jupiter has 63 known moons. The biggest are Ganymede, Io, Europa, and Callisto.

▲ The Great Red Spot on the surface of Jupiter is a never-ending storm. It is more violent than any storms on Earth.

Europa

Europa is the most interesting of Jupiter's **moons**. Why? Because it has **oxygen** and water. These are the two things that life needs to survive.

Europa is rocky. Its surface is covered with frozen water. It is like a huge ice rink. The ice is very thick. It is between 10 kilometres (6 miles) and 50 kilometres (30 miles) thick. It is too deep for you to drill through.

Scientists hope that there is a deep ocean of salty water under the ice. If so, **microbes** and other forms of life could be found down there.

It is extremely cold on Europa (-200 °C; -328 °F). So have a quick skate, and then climb back into your warm spacecraft.

▼ *This cracked ice surface is what Europa might look like. The large **planet** in the background of the photo is Jupiter.*

19

Saturn

Saturn is a giant ball of gas. It is just a bit smaller than Jupiter. Saturn is made mostly of light **hydrogen** gas. So it is very light for its size. If Saturn fell into a large ocean of water, it would float!

Saturn has wide, flat rings around it. You start to fly across the rings. The rings are only 9 metres (30 feet) deep – but they are 480,000 kilometres (300,000 miles) wide. It takes a long time to fly over them.

You cannot land on Saturn. It has thick clouds of hydrogen. Under the clouds is an ocean of liquid hydrogen. Saturn spins around very fast. This whips up winds. The winds are five times stronger than the worst hurricane on Earth!

Saturn

ICY RINGS

Saturn's rings are made mostly of bits of ice. Some bits are as small as snowflakes. Others are as large as a house. The **planets** Jupiter, Uranus, and Neptune also have rings. But Saturn's rings are the brightest.

Titan

You must explore Titan. This is the biggest of Saturn's **moons**. The **atmosphere** (gas) on Titan is mainly **nitrogen** gas. It also has a gas called **methane**.

Life on Earth began about two billion years ago. Titan's atmosphere might be just like Earth's was then. Perhaps you will see the beginning of life here!

Your spacecraft drops down through thick orange clouds. It lands on soft ground. It is almost like sand. Look up! The clouds look green from the ground. There are mountains that look like rock. But they are made of ice. The lakes and rivers are filled with liquid methane – not water! Take samples of everything you find on Titan.

◀ The rivers and lakes on Titan look like water. In fact they are made of liquid methane. You can see Saturn in the sky.

methane gas that is found in rocks
nitrogen type of gas

The farthest planets

Uranus and Neptune

Next stop – the **planet** Uranus. But you will have to travel a long way. Saturn is only halfway from the Sun to Uranus. The next planet, Neptune is nearly twice as far again!

Uranus' and Neptune's **years** are very long. This is because they are far away from the Sun. Uranus takes 84 Earth-years to **orbit** the Sun. Neptune takes 165 Earth-years. Even if you lived 100 Earth-years, you wouldn't reach your first birthday on Neptune!

Uranus

Neptune

PHONING HOME?

Do not think about trying to speak to people back on Earth! It would take 2 hours 45 minutes for the signals to reach Earth from Uranus.

Uranus and Neptune are huge balls of **hydrogen** gas. They are like Jupiter and Saturn, but much smaller. You cannot land on them. You may as well travel on to Pluto, the last planet.

Uranus looks blue. ▶ This is because it is surrounded by frozen clouds of **methane** gas.

◀ Neptune has the strongest winds known. They travel up to 2000 kilometres (1243 miles) per hour.

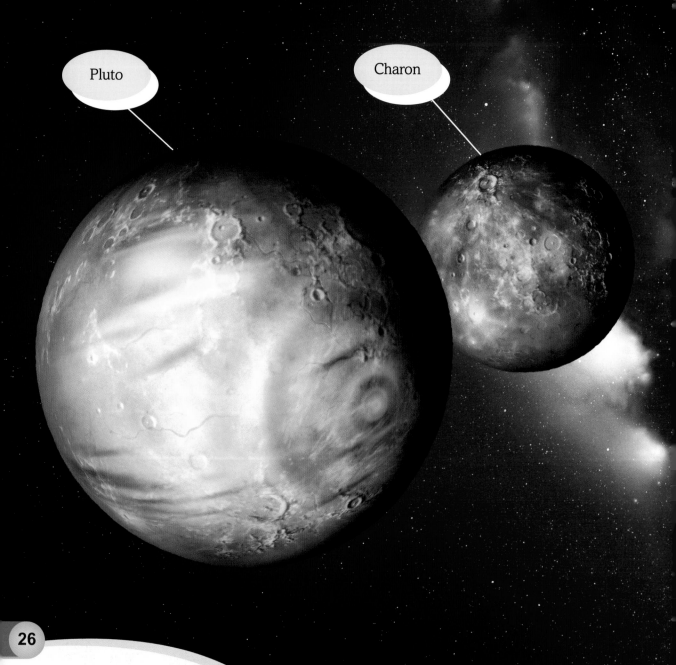

Pluto's moon, Charon, ▲
is not much smaller
than Pluto.

Pluto

If you reach Pluto, you are a very long way from home!
You are also very far from the Sun. From here the Sun
looks like a bright star in the sky.

Pluto is the smallest **planet**. It is also the coldest planet
(-220 °C; -364 °F). Pluto is made of rock. You can land
your spacecraft on it. You will not see much of the Sun
from here. But you will see Pluto's **moon**. It is called
Charon. Charon is almost half the size of Pluto. It will
look huge in Pluto's sky.

Now you must start your journey back to Earth. It
will take you many years to get back. But scientists will
be excited to see you. They want to examine all those
samples you have taken. Who knows, you might have
discovered a tiny alien neighbour!

Pluto

Facts at a glance

The time on this ▶ chart is measured by time on Earth.

Mars

Distance from Sun:
228,000,000 kilometres
(142,000,000 miles)

Spins once in:
24 hours 37 minutes

Orbits the Sun once in:
687 days

Uranus

Distance from Sun:
2871,000,000 kilometres
(1784,000,000 miles)

Spins once in:
17 hours 14 minutes

Orbits the Sun once in:
84 years

Venus

Distance from Sun:
108,000,000 kilometres
(67,000,000 miles)

Spins once in:
243 days

Orbits the Sun once in:
225 days

Neptune

Distance from Sun:
4498,000,000 kilometres
(2795,000,000 miles)

Spins once in:
16 hours

Orbits the Sun once in:
Nearly 165 years

Jupiter

Distance from Sun:
778,000,000 kilometres
(483,000,000 miles)

Spins once in:
9 hours 55 minutes

Orbits the Sun once in:
12 years

Pluto

Distance from Sun:
6000,000,000 kilometres
(3728,000,000 miles)

Spins once in: 6 days 9 hours

Orbits the Sun once in:
Nearly 248 years

Sun

Earth

Distance from Sun:
149,000,000 kilometres
(93,000,000 miles)

Spins once in: 24 hours

Orbits the Sun once in:
365 days (1 year)

Saturn

Distance from Sun:
1429,000,000 kilometres
(888,000,000 miles)

Spins once in:
10 hours 40 minutes

Orbits the Sun once in:
$29\frac{1}{2}$ years

Mercury

Distance from Sun:
58,000,000 kilometres
(36,000,000 miles)

Spins once in: 59 days

Orbits the Sun once in:
88 days

Glossary

asteroid large chunk of rock, or rock and metal, that orbits the Sun.

atmosphere gases that surround a planet or moon.

comet huge icy ball that orbits the Sun.

day length of time it takes for a planet to spin around once.

extinct no longer active.

gravity force that pulls you down to the ground.

hydrogen gas that is much lighter than air. Jupiter, Saturn, Uranus, and Neptune are mainly made of hydrogen.

inner planets the four planets that are nearest to the Sun. These are Mercury, Venus, Earth, and Mars. They are all mainly made of rock.

meteorite lump of rock that drifts through space. When the rock passes close to a planet or moon, gravity pulls it towards the ground.

methane gas that is found in rocks. Methane is made of carbon, hydrogen, and oxygen joined together.

microbe tiny, simple form of life that is too small to see without a microscope. Microbes can survive almost everywhere on Earth, even under thick ice in the Antarctic.

moon object that orbits a planet. The Earth has one natural moon.

nitrogen type of gas. The air on Earth is about four-fifths nitrogen.

orbit to circle around an object.

outer planets the five planets that are farthest from the Sun. These are Jupiter, Saturn, Uranus, Neptune, and Pluto.

oxygen gas that living things need to survive

planet object that orbits the Sun. The Earth is one of nine planets that orbit our Sun.

Solar System the Sun and everything that orbits it. The Solar System includes planets, moons, asteroids, comets, and meteorites.

year length of time it takes a planet to orbit the Sun. All the planets orbit the Sun in the same direction.

Want to know more?

There is lots more to find out about the Solar System. Here are some places to look:

Books to read

- *Encyclopedia of Space*, by Heather Couper and Nigel Henbest (Dorling Kindersley, 2003).

  This book has lots of information about the Solar System, including how the planets were formed and the search for life on Mars.

- *Kingfisher Young Explore: Solar System*, by Mike Goldsmith (Kingfisher, 2004).

  This book tells you more about the Sun, the Moon, and the planets.

Websites

- Heinemann Explore: www.heinemannexplore.co.uk. Everything you need to know about science and history in KS2.

- Starchild: starchild.gsfc.nasa.gov/docs/ StarChild/StarChild.html. A website for children created by NASA, the US space agency.

Gravity is a tricky subject. To find out some amazing things about gravity on Earth, read **10 Experiments Your Teacher Never Told You About**.

There are millions of kinds of microbes – some helpful and some harmful. To find out about some of those that can make you very ill, read **World's Worst Germs**.

Index